BOOKED:
Trip to the Other Side and Back

by
Nancy A. Waldron

Published in the United States of America
First Printing – July 2017
ISBN 978-0-9988383-1-1

Cover design by CrawforDesign | www.crawfordesign.com

Everything

is in

Divine Order

Nancy Waldron and Reggie

Table of Contents

Introduction ix

Chapter 1 .... The Journey Over 1

Chapter 2 .... Exit 1999 – Check In 7

Chapter 3 .... Exit 2016 – Home on the Other Side 13

Chapter 4 .... Radio Show 17

Chapter 5 .... The Journey Back Into the Physical 31

Chapter 6 .... Messages from Home 35

Chapter 7 .... Adjusting to Earth Life 41

Chapter 8 .... Healing Abilities 49

Chapter 9 .... Opportunities 57

Epilogue .... A Heart Filled with Gratitude 61

Resources 66

A note about the title: Debbie Smith, a Medium friend of mine, said it was like Spirit said, "Let's book her a trip to Tokyo, no, let's book her a trip to the Other Side." Thus, the title "Booked: Trip to the Other Side and Back."

Introduction

I wrote this to be helpful to those who wonder about what goes on before, during, and after you go to the Other Side. My experience unfolded slowly after I returned and experiences continue to merge in now. My life is richer and fuller than it has ever been because of the strength of my connection with, and the experiences I had on, the Other Side.

While writing this book, I would go into an altered state and write away for hours. It is such a pleasant place to be that I loved going to my computer after my normal morning routine to connect in with Spirit. I had to be careful not to go too far out of my body. If I would start to get the feeling that I was leaving, I would stop writing, and play with my little dog, Reggie, or go out in the garden to take a walk and ground back into Earth life with nature.

It totally and completely surprised me that my heart had stopped. I have been healthy most of my adult life. I had a number of common and uncommon childhood illnesses. I exercise every day, lift weights, take a brisk walk, take vitamins, and eat healthy.

I have been on the spiritual path my whole life, well except for a detour or two, and am self-monitoring, strive to be positive, and allow only uplifting books, movies, and people in my life where possible.

After this experience, it changed my connection with the Other Side. I now possess a certainty that I am enfolded with Spirit every moment. Spirit guides my every thought and word with surprising things coming out of my mouth. My actions are authentic even though it takes me time to understand what Spirit wants from me. I feel whole in a way that is complete in every moment. I am not looking forward or backward; I am present in this moment. It is all I have.

Two of the chapters which talk about my trips to the Other Side are titled Exit 1999 and Exit 2016. These came from driving for many years in the Los Angeles area with the many freeway exits. I have come to think of my journey as having Exits similar to those on a freeway. There are exit points in life where we can choose to return to the Other Side for a check in and come back, or stay on the Other Side.

I trust you will enjoy this book as much as I enjoyed the Journey.

Nancy A. Waldron

CHAPTER 1
The Journey Over

It was Monday of Thanksgiving week, November 21, 2016, around 9:30 pm. I was watching TV and thinking about my trip to Redding the next morning to see my friend and her dog. I had picked up some Chinese food for dinner that evening since I didn't want to cook and leave food in the refrigerator while I was gone.

My stomach began to feel a little queasy, my bowels a little like I had to go, and I thought there must have been something in the food that wasn't good. I started for the bathroom and in the hall, something affected me like a blow to my body. I knew I was going to faint, so I lay down on the bathroom floor and passed out.

While I was lying there in and out of consciousness, I was aware that I was in a concrete room. I thought I needed to call my friend, Cherry, then knew I was not to do that. Cherry is a very clear Medium who communicates with spirits on the Other Side. A few days later, I was telling Cherry about my experiences. She told me that around that same time she was asleep, and that she had a dream where she saw a man and a woman in a concrete room. She "got" that the man was her brother, but couldn't make out who the woman was. She knew someone was going to die and thought it was her brother. After I told her about my experience, she knew the woman was me and I was the one who died. We are so closely connected spiritually that it did not surprise me when she said that as I had called her with my thoughts. You will read more about this experience in another chapter.

I came to as I lay on the floor, and my liquid body fluid had eliminated on the floor. My bowels were ready to eliminate, so I got up and sat on the toilet. I thought I had food poisoning. I went to the family room, turned off the TV and lights, got my cell phone and went to my bedroom with my little dog, Reggie. I put on my nightgown and lay down. I felt so sick and had to go to the bathroom again. My bowels again eliminated. It was like a faucet turning on rather than like my normal bowel activity. As I was on the toilet, I knew I was going to faint again, so lay down on the floor.

I had enough presence of mind to take my cell phone with me when I went into the bathroom. When I came to, I called my neighbor, Heather, and asked her to check on me later as I wasn't feeling well. She insisted on coming over right then with her husband, Kal. His name is Khalid, but I call him Kal. She had a key so she could get in the house when I am gone and if my little Reggie needs anything.

She came back to the bathroom to see if I had on clothing, then called her husband to come. Kal came in, squatted down, took my hand, patted it, and told me everything was going to be alright. He told Heather to call 911, which she did. Kal asked me if I wanted to notify someone and I told him I hated to bother anyone. He was persistent and so I had him call my son, Wayne, to let him know what was going on.

Barbara, my sister, had the legal authority to act if I was unable to, but she was having company the next day and I didn't want to disturb her. I thought it was food poisoning and not a big deal. Wayne called her to tell her what was going on after Kal called him.

I lay there until the Paramedics came. I am guessing I passed out again as I do not remember anything until one of them asked me if I could walk. I told him no, but I could crawl. I crawled to an office chair with wheels on it, and they lifted me in the chair.

When the Paramedics came, my little Reggie got so upset as he knew something was very wrong with me. He started licking my face and crying while I was laying on the floor. The Paramedics asked that the dog be removed. Kal asked Heather to take him over to their house. We have a wonderful arrangement where we keep each other's dog when we need to be gone. They have a little dog, Teddy, and he and Reggie love each other and play together often.

When the Paramedics started moving me down the hall, one of them told me to lift up my feet so they didn't drag. I am 6' tall, so have a long body. While they were pushing me down the hall, I passed out again. I do not know how they got me to the stretcher. The next thing I remember is one of the Paramedics asking me if I had ever had heart trouble and I said no. I thought to myself that maybe that's what is wrong with my body and not food poisoning. I also remember the Paramedic said, *"Stay with me, Nancy."*

On the Emergency Notification Sheet taped up on my refrigerator, I have "DO NOT RESUSCITATE, Advanced Directive, HIPAA, and Living Will in effect." I was told that the Paramedic asked me if I wanted to be revived and I said yes. I have no memory of that but am happy he asked. I am guessing they used the paddles to jump start my heart at the house and on the way. Everything in my body hurt!

They took me to the Emergency Room at Sutter Auburn Faith Hospital in Auburn, CA, where the doctor and nurses worked on me for hours. I have no memory of the ride. Once in the ER, I threw up all the remaining contents of my stomach at the hospital a couple of times, then had dry heaves. My temperature dropped and I was freezing cold. They cut off my nightgown and wrapped me in an air bubble package that heated my body. I remember telling the nurses a few times that I was so sick. One of the nurses said: "We are doing everything we can for you." I thanked her.

I believe I had an X-ray taken at one point. Moving caused my heart to stop. One of the nurses came to tell me that my sister was coming. My heart eased as she and I are so close. I could feel that she was so worried and afraid I wouldn't make it until she got there. She called periodically to check on my status.

My daughter-in-law, Nikki, is a nurse so she was on the phone with the ER nurses providing them with the medications I was allergic to. I had prepared a sheet for Barbara and each of the kids in the event of illness or death, outlining who my doctors were, what medications I was allergic to, and how to contact everyone involved. Wayne had efficiently filed it so it could be pulled out quickly and then had Nikki relay the information.

The ER nurses had me reclining with my torso upright. Once I opened my eyes and looked out the ER door to the waiting area and saw my dear neighbor, Kal, sitting there. It surprised and touched me that he was so loving he would be waiting. He stayed with me in the Emergency Room until 2:00 am, when my heart stabilized. He told me later he didn't want me to be alone. How very precious he is! Without him and Heather, I would now be on the Other Side. There are no accidents. Everything is in Divine Order!

Kal later told me that Reggie was so upset, he threw up and had diarrhea, and it took a long time of holding him, petting him, and telling him I was going to be alright before he settled down. They kept Reggie until I came home from the hospital. I can never thank him and Heather enough for their love and care of both Reggie and me.

Kal told me that my heart stopped four times in the hospital. He didn't think I was going to make it, but he kept praying for me.

I had IV's on each arm, tubes for every purpose, oxygen, and I don't know what else. Once my heart stabilized early the next morning, I was taken by Critical Care Ambulance down to the Cardiac Care Unit at Sutter General Hospital in Roseville. Later that morning, Dr. George Fehrenbacher, M.D., F.A.C.C., a Cardiology Doctor, implanted a Pacemaker. He told me I did not have a heart attack, my heart simply stopped due to a blockage.

My neighbor, Heather Jaber wrote the following account of her and Khalid's (Kal) personal experience the night my heart stopped. I'm sharing it with you as it has details I was not aware of. It has been edited slightly for clarity.

"After receiving the initial call from Nancy, Khalid and I grabbed her house key and proceeded to her house. Initially, we knocked to see if Nancy opened. After knocking, Reggie came to the door and proceeded to continuously bark in an urgent manner. At this point, Khalid and I used her key and entered the home. Reggie anxiously barked and ran around in circles, barking and leading me back to the master bathroom, where Nancy was lying on the ground. Khalid remained at the front door until I could verify that Nancy was fully clothed."

"Khalid proceeded to join me in the bathroom, where he directed me to call 911. Once both Khalid and I were with Nancy, Reggie immediately settled on the bed and waited. While I phoned 911, Khalid knelt down on the ground next to Nancy and took her hand, while I was on the phone, Khalid proceeded to stroke her hand and gently reassure Nancy that she was going to be okay and to stay with him. Once 911 was dispatched, we questioned Nancy about who needed to be notified. After direction from Nancy, I made phone calls, while Khalid continued to speak to Nancy and keep her engaged until the paramedics arrived. We spoke with Wayne and his wife, the RN as Nancy has noted."

"Once the paramedics arrived, Reggie immediately jumped from the bed and went to Nancy. The paramedics asked me to remove him. I took Reggie from the room, while Khalid remained with Nancy. The entire time Nancy was in and out of consciousness. Reggie easily followed me out of the room, after which I helped the paramedic move rugs and get a rolling chair to roll her out to the stretcher. The paramedic took her Do Not Resuscitate orders from the refrigerator, and asked me to please verify them with her when she was conscious again. I had told him that she was in and out of consciousness."

"I grabbed Reggie's stuffed toy and took Reggie to our home, placed

him with our dog Ted and reassured him that Nancy would be okay and that he would stay with us until she came home. Khalid remained by Nancy's side and assisted the paramedics. Once she was on the stretcher and in the ambulance, the paramedic asked if family had been notified, to which we said yes and gave the information we had. They said they were taking her to Auburn Faith. Khalid didn't want Nancy to be alone and decided to follow the ambulance."

"Upon arrival at the hospital, Khalid was informed that each time Nancy lost consciousness, her heart was actually stopping. Khalid can't remember how many times she was resuscitated, but stated she was resuscitated in the ambulance and several times in the ER. He recalls seeing and hearing the electric paddles and nurses scurrying about at least four times. Because Nancy's heart was stopping, her body was eliminating waste, so out of respect for Nancy's modesty, Khalid sat in a chair outside of her room, hoping she would feel that someone was with her. Khalid also knew that when the body began to eliminate waste, such as what Nancy was doing, that she was dying. He was fearful she wouldn't make it and continued to pray for her to stabilize."

"Once they were able to stabilize Nancy and her family was taking over the involvement, Khalid left the ER at about 2:00 am in the morning. We were told that Nancy would need a pacemaker and that her sister was making arrangements to fly out. We made arrangements to keep Reggie with us until Nancy returned home. We are so grateful that we were able to help and that Nancy was able to make a full recovery."

This was the second time I left my body (Exit 2016 for the year 2016), and went to the Other Side. This triggered the memory of the first time I left my body in 1999, which I call Exit 1999.

CHAPTER 2
Exit 1999, My first Check In

Each person has exit points in their life when they can crossover to the Other Side. One of my exit points was in August of 1999. Bill and I had just come back from a trip to Colorado Springs to meet with my family. My father left his half of a 2500-acre farm corporation to the family after he died in 1998. My mother and sisters wanted to sell it; I did and did not. I could see the problems that would crop up with who would manage it, and the egos, etc. that would be involved. My younger sister lived in Colorado Springs, my older sister lived in Denver, and Bill and I lived in Bella Vista, CA.

Bill and I had come back to help my dad with harvest for years. I felt I was the only one of the sisters genuinely interested in the farm, land and all that went with it. They preferred city living to the quiet of the farm. My older sister would do what I call "pretend" to love the farm, talking a good game but usually too busy with her work to go out there. Once in a great while she would go to gain favor with my father, I thought. My younger sister was honest about her feelings and went when she genuinely wanted to, but didn't curry favor with my father. I called my sisters mother's daughters; I considered myself my father's daughter. Mother was outraged that I would question her decision and felt the farm was hers only as did my sisters. She would not talk to me about it directly, which was her pattern over the years. Her word was law in the family when I was a child, but not over me when I became an adult.

I didn't share their opinion since it was a corporation and we were all on the Board of Directors and, on paper I was appointed as Assistant Manager. I considered it to be all of ours. I also felt I had earned it; I didn't sit on my backside and do nothing. From the time I was old enough to be of any use, I washed dishes, helped prepare and serve meals to the family, other family members, guests of the folks, and many farm and harvest hands. I helped clean the house, did the wash and ironing, and whatever needed to be done for Mother. On the farm, we had outhouses for toilets, water was hauled inside in a bucket and boiled on a stove that was fed by wood, irons were heated on the top of the stove for ironing and so forth.

During my childhood and until I left home, I went with my dad when I could and helped him with greasing machinery, handing him tools in the barn when he worked repairing equipment, filling the planting machinery with wheat, etc. When I was older, I would help with harvest and drive whatever equipment I could that would help him. I loved being with him as he was kind and taught me in a gentle manner. When he was older and could no longer climb to the top of the grain bins, I would climb up to close the hatch when a storm was coming.

The farm was the legacy so lovingly gifted to us by our father, who had worked his life to acquire and give us all this incredible gift of ongoing crops/income and valuable land. On one hand, I believed it could have provided us all with extras, a place to go if we ever needed it, and especially since everything was in place for its continued operation. On the other hand, I also knew that it would be difficult for Bill and I to manage the farm from California. Neither of us genuinely wanted to move back to Colorado.

I had the intuitive knowing that if I wanted to keep it, Mother would dig in on selling it. I intuited that she perceived it was only hers and she would make the decision. The corporation was just paper. She knew my sisters would do whatever she wanted.

In July of 1999, Bill and I went back to Colorado Springs to talk with the family to try to ease tensions. They would only meet with us at their CPA's office, which was fine with me as I knew Mother would act differently there than if we were at home. We met and opinions were stated. My older sister was openly hostile, was Mother's spokesperson, and was highly judgmental of me. Mother declined to say anything and wrapped herself in the cloak of martyr. She was a master at being a martyr. My younger sister and her husband didn't say much. The CPA outlined the tax consequences and other pertinent bits of information. As Bill and I left, I looked at my younger sister and told her the name of someone who wanted to buy the land, if they decided to sell. I felt they had shut me/us out of the family circle, out of their homes, and out of their lives because I would not agree with selling.

I went home and wrote a letter to everyone who knew about Dad's death and his wishes to pass on the farm, asking them to speak to Mother about not selling the farm. This was like throwing gasoline on a fire and had consequences for me that were, and are, lifelong. My mother was mortified, my older sister furious, and my younger sister despairing of yet another family crisis.

Retrospectively, I can see where my thoughts were divisive, let alone my actions. I knew I could have just let things be, never said a word, and played along with the family game of "Mother's always right." That wasn't who I was nor would I have learned so much if I had.

Inside, I was sick at heart that my family would shut me out for having a different opinion and speaking up about it. Sometimes, it was my pattern to say what I thought within the family regardless of the consequences. Before I ever said or did anything, I knew when I went against what Mother wanted to do, she would cut me out of her will, and she did. My soul could not be bought for money; it wasn't for sale.

After we got home to Bella Vista, I went to breakfast a couple of days later with my friend, Shirley, who sees and communicates with Spirits. As we were sitting at breakfast, I started to feel bad and went to the restroom. I came back and continued to visit a bit more, then told Shirley that I didn't feel well and I needed to lay down. She said if I lay down on the ground they would have to call the Paramedics. I told her I couldn't help it and lay down. I crossed over almost all the way. The liquid fluids drained out of my body. When the Paramedics got there, I had no heartbeat, no pulse, and no respiration. While they were working on me, Shirley saw a Being show me a tablet that held what I had committed to accomplish before I crossed over completely. I came back into my body. I was taken to the hospital and tests run. I knew they would find nothing wrong with me. I knew I had just had taken Exit '99 and then returned.

I did not bring back conscious memories of my meeting with the Beings on the Other Side: the family members and Off-Planet Beings or The Council. I brought back a peacefulness and an inner strength to continue on with or without the family. I brought back an awareness that family are those who genuinely support you for who you are, differing opinions and all. I had always thought of family as those in my biological lineage; i.e., my parents, grandparents, aunts, uncles, cousins, and so forth. After my time on the Other Side, my definition of family expanded to include not only biological family members who genuinely supported me, but also close friends and those who choose to share my spiritual journey. The experience expanded my awareness about myself, my biological family, my soul family, and contact with the Other Side.

Sometime later, I asked myself if it was worth it. After pondering it for some time, I knew that it was, as I supported myself as a soul with my own opinion and worth. It changed me and the dynamics of the family as I took a break from them completely for two or three years. My younger sister and I continued to have some occasional contact as she is simply loving.

During the next few months, I wrote and published my first book, *A Joyful Miracle, How I made my father's death a joyful miracle and how you can plan for this too*. As with this book, I sat down at the computer and it flowed through me with ease.

The writing and all of the details involved in publishing the book went like clockwork. It was all in Divine Order!

Most of my life, I was under the impression that I had to "make things happen." I believed that if I didn't make things happen, nothing did. I left little room for Spirit to assist, nor did I know at times when Spirit did assist. I would just push and push until something was done, exhausting myself in the process. I learned that there is my part to do and as soon as I know what that is, I do it willingly. I learned to wait for Spirit to give me a sign or guidance. I also learned that if something is supposed to be, it will flow smoothly and easily. If it isn't, I just let it go as something better is coming along. This is a lesson I learned that improved my life and brought relaxation to my body, mind, and spirit.

CHAPTER 3
Exit 2016, Home on the Other Side

While all of this was going on in the hospital, I did, in fact, die and crossover completely to the Other Side. I was aware that initially I was surrounded by foggy White Light, that my deceased husband, Bill, was there along with other family members, as well as what I call "The Council." They appeared as Bright Lights in the distance in the foggy White Light. It was Exit 2016 for me.

About a month or so earlier, I had written my sisters each a letter telling them how much I loved our life together, thanked them for being my sisters and all their help over the years. I wanted them to know how much I loved them and how much they meant to me.

I felt like I had completed my life in many ways as I had a good relationship with my sisters, and my children were all in good places. I had taken care of Bill for eight years before he crossed over, planned and had his Celebration of Life service, and completed all of the death details. My grandchildren had all graduated from high school or had graduated from college. I had moved to Auburn, CA, after Bill died to be in a less stressful, small community, had met people, had a church family, and had established a comfortable life for myself.

In December of 2015, I received the information from Spirit that this was someone's last Christmas. I asked if it was mine and was told "no." At the time, I thought it was my older sister as she was having some health issues. So, I let it go and knew if I was to know, the information would be given to me. When my heart stopped, I thought it was me that Spirit had given me advance knowledge that it would be my last Christmas, even though they said "no".

When I was a child, I fainted quite a bit. If I didn't like what was going on I simply left my body. They would or wouldn't find anything wrong with me. This continued even after I was married. I simply went to the Other Side where I was loved unconditionally and cared for, and left what I didn't like. I knew what I was doing. I got in the habit of leaving my body, a more expanded version of "flight" rather than fight response. It was my private exit that no one else here in the physical consciously knew about.

Back in the ER while they continued to work on me, I was busy on the Other Side. Since there is no time on the Other Side, I experienced all these things happening simultaneously. My awareness of these events unfolded over time. Upon arriving on the Other Side, I was immersed in the greatest Love/Light. I knew I was home. It was foggy at first then the Light got brighter as the Love increased until I was the Light/Love merged back with Source. It is an indescribable feeling of beyond bliss unlike anything on Earth. I was merged with Bill, my parents, my pets, other family members, friends, lands and galaxies, planets and areas of the Cosmos I love, and The Council.

Everything is there that I love, and more – the atmosphere, the colors, the music, the sounds, the smells. Here on Earth, I love the mystical interlude, the time just at dawn and just at sunset, when there is a stillness, a deep silence as it is a time I love to connect with the Other Side. I love the luminescent colors of the rainbow that are so vibrant and yet soft on the Other Side. The music fills me and lifts me to the greatest love. The sounds I love of the flowing stream, the breeze rustling, the forest, the birds, and so much more are in me. The smells that nurture me here on Earth, the Stargazer Lilies, roses, the Earth after a rain, freshly plowed ground, my little dog's outdoor smell after he comes in, and all that I bring to myself here on this plane are there effortlessly. It is part of being enfolded in and merging with Home. I love to dance here on Earth and when I dance, I AM the dance. I merge with the music, the movement, the energy, vibration, and frequency of all of it blended together. When I am in that space, I feel as if I am floating when I dance. On the Other Side, it is all merged together in a very, very fine flow that is difficult to describe, put precious beyond measure to experience.

Before we incarnate into life, each of us outlines what we agree to accomplish and when we expect to complete what we agreed to do. Agreements can be changed as can time lines. While on the Other Side, I merged with my life agreement to this point and could see that I had completed what I came to do. The old patterns of my early childhood training were removed by both my mother's and father's side of the family. Areas that I had been closed off and guarded about were opened up. They all infused me with wisdom about my life, life on the Other Side, and the life I would have upon return to my physical body.

As I live each day now, something new unfolds that wasn't there before. When I walk, I am consciously aware that I am walking through energy, vibrations, and frequencies. At times, it feels like Light waves, and other times it feels like thick, dense energy. I feel the energies and vibrations on my physical legs and sense the frequencies with my ears. It is interesting because it doesn't disturb my normal balance or Beingness. I am just aware of much more going on.

My grandson, Keith, just graduated from college, and there was a party for him. At the end of the party, I had prepared some things I wanted to say to his parents about what a wonderful job each of them had done, and they had done together. I started speaking and got about half-way through, when I felt this incredibly beautiful fine flow of pure love flow into me. The tears started falling at the beauty of the love that was coming through me and into each person in the room. It was so deeply touching that I cried through the rest of the words. It was the ending to raising a son from a baby to a man, and the new chapters that would unfold in the parents and son's lives. It was a blessing upon all there from Spirit.

This happens to me a lot when I speak in front of groups as Spirit flows a level of love through me that opens the majority of people. There are times that I am crying for those in the group who cannot cry at the beauty of feelings. It used to embarrass me as I wanted to be so professional, now I enfold the grace of being a vehicle for this level of love to flow through. Before my second trip to the Other Side, I felt more human and connected in with Spirit. After my second trip to the Other Side, I am blended, merged with the Other Side as one.

CHAPTER 4

The Radio Show

On Wednesday, December 14, 2016, two and a half weeks after I came home from the hospital, Cherry Divine was visiting me and had to do the "Something Brewin" Blog Talk Radio Show that morning. She asked me if I would be a guest and talk about my experience. I said sure I would. She hosts the show with Tracie Mahan every Wednesday at 7:00 am Pacific Time, and they talk about different spiritual topics, answer questions, and do readings for callers and those in the Chat Room.

I was a little bit anxious as it had been a while since I was on a radio show. I didn't know if I would know what to say. Then while I was talking on the show, it was so easy and the words just flowed from my mouth. When listening to it some months later, I marveled at the knowledge I had and the manner in which I spoke, clear, certain, and with a precision that was new to me. It was surreal! I share this with you as it shows how my connection with the Other Side just flows. Cherry's and Tracie's input was invaluable also.

The following are edited excerpts, in part, from the radio show.

Cherry: *Nancy Waldron had a pretty amazing experience. Her heart stopped, not just once, not twice, but four times. They used the paddles to restart her heart in her home and on the way to the hospital. Later it was determined that she needed a Pacemaker. Nancy is going to talk with us today about her death experience. Shall we welcome Nancy Waldron everybody!*

Nancy: *Good Morning. Thank you for having me on the show. It was quite an interesting experience and, actually, quite a life changing experience. I am going to just back up a little bit and tell you what I did before I had this experience, I had written my sisters letters and told them how much I loved them. I had completed many things and had the awareness that something was going to happen. I didn't know what. I thought maybe I am moving to a different state, or whatever. And then when my heart stopped, I realized that this was an exit point for me, that I could have passed over and just stayed on the Other Side. But I did not.*

What happened the first time that I remember my heart stopping and coming back was, I was in a concrete room. It was a gray concrete room and I knew it was concrete. Then I came back into consciousness in the bathroom where I was laying on the floor. I got myself up, got my phone and thought I better go to bed so I would feel better. The next time I passed out, I'm in a different bathroom on the floor, and I don't know whether it was this time or one of the other times that I crossed over. Because I did crossover completely. I was in like an opaque light and I saw other lights at the end of that light, and I had the awareness that my deceased husband was over lighting the whole process. I had some memory of what happened here at the house and I don't have any memory of the ride to the hospital. In the hospital, I know I was deathly ill. I remembered that it was hard for me to decide to come back, which was interesting. I knew that I chose to come back because I have more work that I agreed to do here.

Cherry: *You know what was interesting, not to interrupt Nancy, at the time she had her first heart stopping where she was on the bathroom floor, I was already in bed asleep. All of a sudden in my dreams, I was in a big empty warehouse, concrete walls, and there was a female figure off to my left. I couldn't really see her and I knew she wasn't a solid body. And then my brother was on the other side and in it he had a box that he had sat down that was just jumbled with junk. I told him, you cannot leave that mess here, you have to pick it up and take it with you. And the whole time, I knew this woman was there and watching us, and I woke up instantly and thought what is this dream. What I didn't know is that Nancy thought she was passing out, but her heart was actually stopping. And so, when she went to the concrete room, apparently, she contacted me. She ended up in a concrete room. In my mind now I understand it was her; at that time, I didn't know it was her. I just knew it was a woman figure, surrounded by light and she was watching. So, this is really interesting how when we do move through the transition, many times many people will go straight over, but others linger and make decisions and choices, and will contact others. There are many of us who have had people who are getting ready to cross over contact us before they die.*

Nancy: *On that note, I had tried to call Cherry a couple of times on the weekend before that happened, and she wasn't available. I had a knowing that if I contacted her and said how I was feeling, it would have shifted things just a little bit. The other part of the story is I was scheduled to drive to Redding, California the next morning to spend Thanksgiving with a friend. Before I even left here, that afternoon or evening, I am not sure of the timing here, I had the premonition that if anything happened, the husband has connections to the medical. I had the thought flash through me that they can help me. So, it was a choice as to whether or not I was going to have the experience in my own home, in my own town, or whether I was going to have the experience up in Redding. There were several little caveats here that played into this before and after.*

They moved me to a hospital that had cardiac care, The Pacemaker was implanted the next morning. I have been aware since then that I have a totally calm demeanor. I also am aware that the next time I go, I won't come back. Many things have been coming into play that my awareness brings back to me on different levels at different times since I've come back. This has been an interesting journey before, during, and after the experience.

Tracie: *Can I ask a question real quick?*

Nancy: *Sure*

Tracie: *How does that change your view of death and dying?*

Nancy: *I actually don't have any view of death and dying, I am just moving to another dimension. Frankly, since I've been a child, I've spent a lot of time crossing over and coming back, but not entirely leaving the body. I entirely left the body one other time, and a friend was with me. She saw a being who was showing me a tablet so I came back in time. This time I went, and I am pretty certain that my deceased husband was instrumental in helping me see what all I needed to, not needed, but could assist with on many levels. So, I made a choice to come back.*

Cherry: *Something I do want to bring up is, when Nancy came back, she was still connected to the Other Side and there is this wonderful euphoric feeling. You get to feel the infiniteness of all life and see it, yet not be attached to the emotional body of the human experience. You can go through some sadness and I talked to her a day or two afterwards. She was very sad and she didn't understand, just crying and that sort of thing. It reminded me that years ago when my middle granddaughter was born and the first day she was born I thought this is really good. The next day I had this unbearable sadness and I am asking "is this all there is?". If this is all there is, then I don't want to be here. Nancy was talking with me about this, about this wasn't enough. When you touch on it, and this is the thing with newborn babies and near-death experiences, you get to feel that energy. The newborns bring that energy in and it gives you this sense of longing to be in that expanded form, not to be tied down into the feeling of weightedness in the human experience. Yet as Nancy and I talked, it was very clear, she was not done and her body had to be reconfigured to be able to hold the shift of energy in her body, the shift of light in her body. I can tell you, just feeling her vibration – and she has always been a high being since I've known her - but there still has been a significant change.*

Nancy: *Yes, and I feel that change; I feel it on a physical level, on a cellular level. I feel my body differently. I feel that I am eating differently. I am thinking differently. I have always been a fast-paced person. I like to do things quickly and easily and just accomplish a lot. I feel that I have settled into a calmer, a much, not slower, a more deliberate, a more – I call it Divine Order - pace to my life. I am not in a hurry. I know that things are unfolding for me and for all of those around me in a way and at a pace that will change them, everybody I have contact with. They seem to be aware of it as they comment to me about "oh you seem so much different and you seem like you are in a really calm place." And I said, "yes, I am."*

Tracie: *You said that you had a near death experience, so you have been coming and going out of your body and that sounds like that is just an ability that you were born with to move through those dimensions?*

Nancy: *Yes*

Tracie: *It sounded like you had another near-death experience where you had a choice to come back as a younger person.*

Nancy: *Right, it was in 2002 or 2004, something along that line. I was at a restaurant and I was eating and then I just started not feeling well. I told my friend, I have to lay down. My friend said if you lay down, they are going to call the paramedics. I had to lay down and they did call the paramedics. When the paramedics came, I had no heartbeat, no pulse, and my bodily fluids had released. They brought me back. They took me to the hospital and, of course, they could not find anything wrong, which I knew they wouldn't. That time, my intent was to leave the body. I had had something happen with the biological family that I just said, I am not going to stay, I am leaving. That is it, I am done.*

Tracie: *I know how to exit, I am out of here.*

Nancy: *Joking and laughing, I said: Right, don't mess with me, I am out of here. When people say they are out of here, they don't literally know that when I say I am out of here, I mean out of here. It is not just I am leaving going out the door. I came back from that and again I came back with a very calm demeanor. I knew that I had things to do, I went right ahead with my life, and things evolved and changed, and I went on a path that was much deeper, much purer, and of the Divine. So, it was very meaningful.*

Tracie: *So it was easier once you came back? Do you think that you just kind of came back with that knowing that you have a purpose here, you have things that you intended to do while you were here, and as you came back, was it easier to be here even though you had reasons to want to check out?*

Nancy: *Yes, it was, because for some reason whatever happened on the Other Side, it gave me the view that I was the one changing the dynamics of the whole family. I was the one changing the dynamics of the friends around me, and I needed to not run from that experience, if you will. I needed to stay and hold to that so that what I was bringing in would uplift and expand and activate the people around me. So, it was totally different from this time. That time brought me back with family and friends and things I needed to do around them, and I wasn't complete. This time I could have stayed on the Other Side and I made the choice to come back. So that was the difference between the first time and this time, in that the first time it was a choice for me to go check in then. That wasn't an exit point; this time was an exit point and I chose to come back.*

Tracie: *Wow, I do have another question. So, you went through the experience of the first near death experience to get to know what it was like to be on the Other Side, came back because you had things to do. If it happens to you again, you check out, you have that near death experience, what will you do? I was told before that we have different check out points, all of us do. We have a choice to go then or keep going here, and there can be five different check out points. You will just check in and either opt for another level or like you did with the near-death experiences, those were check out points for you or how does that work?*

Nancy: *For me, I felt like it was a check out point. The first one was a choice check in/out point, but I wasn't done and I knew it. You know how people have a tantrum because they don't want to do something any more. I didn't like what is going on so I thought I am not going to do this anymore. The first one was that kind of a thing. From that I brought back a level of maturity spiritually. This time was a definite check out point and so it was different in that, yes,*

I could have, but no I chose not to because I chose to help in ways that are beyond any awareness that I had prior to this.

Tracie: *Wow, I always find this stuff so fascinating. I really do appreciate that you came on today to share all this with us. So, what is the driving force now, now that you came back again and obviously there is still more to do. So, what do you know about that?*

Nancy: *The first time I left, I came back and there was more that I was going to do, in a doing sense. This time when I came back, it is more "being". My Beingness, if you will, is what is assisting all. I can do things like I've just completed a little booklet called **My Spiritual Journey and Yours**, and I am publishing that, but it is not that. It is my Beingness, the Light I carry within. I have had the awareness that the old light was taken out and I was infused with a new and greater light. That when you walk by me, when I go places, when I am just sitting in my house, I am emanating and radiating out a different light, a different level of essence than I was before. So, it is my Beingness, rather than my doingness, that is the difference.*

Tracie: *Wow, I love that.*

Cherry: *I do want to say a couple of things really quick. First of all, I for one, am happy that Nancy decided she wanted to come back. I think there were several of us that were holding her. Reggie barks saying, no, no, we are not letting her go. Also, I want to talk a little bit about the exit points. I have the understanding that there may be many exit points that abound. Yet I agree with Nancy that there are times we go up and do a check in. But from the understanding I have, we set about many different exit points. And I have had a couple come very close to me, yet we may decide not to go then. But from what my group tells me, we do plan one final one that we do not turn back from. It isn't that we cannot rewrite our agreements, but for the most part we are saying no this is where we actually choose to leave the physical body for the final time. So, it is as if there are way points, the group is showing like rest stops along the way. We can either get back on the highway or we can just stay there and move in a different direction.*

Tracie: *We do have a couple of questions in the Chat Room about the near-death experience as well, so let me read one here. 'Why is it that only some people can recall a near death experience, I had a near miss, but I don't recall anything.' So, is that true that only some people are recalling the near death experience?*

Cherry: *You know, Tracie, as soon as you were reading hers, what I got is, it is the same thing with visitation. We will have these and they will seem as if we don't hold the memories, yet we do. They are telling me that in the interfacing of who we are, that we may not have a conscious memory of it, but when we check in it stays in our interfacing. I have never had that one come up before. Many times, it will point us in a different direction, or open up a direction that we were headed, or create a new aware understanding. So, when you have these, also pay attention to any changes in development in your life around you, or all of a sudden, it is a different perception, or an understanding, or awareness. Because I do get that she has a memory of her experience, but it stays in the background until she is fully ready for all of the information to come in.*

Tracie: *Nancy, did you have anything else to add to that.*

Nancy: *I wanted to add one other thing and that is all those connecting in and all of those who have any interest in near death experiences, or have experiences that they haven't known, we are connecting. I am sending out my essence, the Light that I received on this last crossover. I am sending it out to them so that they can become more aware and more comfortable with the fact that this is kind of like crossing the street. That it is OK if you don't remember. You don't have to hide from the information, that it will come up more easily when you are ready. This kind of work is the work that I am doing. I don't call it work, I don't have a name for it because it is like an over lighting of humanity, if you will, to give them the inner peace, the inner joy of saying 'Yes, this is what I know. Yes, this is who I am. I am that beautiful, beautiful Divine Being that can know more'.*

Tracie: *Yes, that is a neat thing to know, very precious. OK, so there is another question in here. ' Presuming the brain is dead during the near-death experience, how does the brain remember what occurred during that near-death experience?'*

Nancy: *We have technical terms where the medical community will declare someone brain dead and that they are dead bodily, if you will. However, Spirit keeps the physical body going until a decision is made. They kept my physical body even though the medical community was doing all that they could do, because there was a point at which in the emergency room, they said we don't know what else to do. Spirit kept my physical body, my Beingness on this plane, in a state that I could come back into it without any damage, without any disturbance of any of the systems, and actually an upgrade of the systems. So that is how Spirit does it for some. I don't know that they do it for all, because there may be other lessons that someone is to learn. For instance, if you come back and you can't remember anything, then maybe your lesson is that you don't need to remember. All you need to do is immerse yourself in your present life.*

Tracie: *Yeah, very true.*

Cherry: *Yes, and there is another part too, and that is remembering the physical body being held by Spirit and being held in a place of safety, that your soul is always alive. Another woman had a near death experience and one of the things she talks about is when she left her body, she was aware of everything going on. And this has been my understanding for many, many years is all of a sudden you are seeing the tapestry of life. And again, it is different for different people and different writings will give different experiences. But here she is, she was above her body, she is seeing everything that is going on in the hospital room, in where she had died, she felt everybody's emotions. She felt her parents. Her brother was in an airplane coming over, she could feel his worry, would he make it in time. She saw why her path was the way it was, why every intermixing, every connection with any and all physical people. Again, there was a larger understanding that came in. Our physical bodies and the idea of the brain isn't the only thing that we rely on in this life. It is part of who we are, but it is the soul, the essence of who you are and the life force that you are that holds much more information. Every cell in your body, every particle of light that you are carries information whether it be of this life or any other life. So again, it is really important to allow yourself to just to open to look at many, many potentials and possibilities. And the Heart Chakra carries huge memory.*

Tracie: *We will go back to the blog talk and we have a question.*

Nancy: *Tracie, if I may add another thing, one of the benefits that I have been experiencing and witnessing from my crossover and come back, is that I have opened hearts at a greater level in a greater way than had ever been opened before. I brought people to an awareness that if you are in this physical body, there is a time limit and that things that you want to do, and things you want to say, relationships you want to mend, and so forth, it is now. There is only this moment – it is now, and so that helped many people move on. It was like a shock wave going through family and friends because I have been extremely healthy. I exercise, I lift weights, I go ballroom dancing. You know, I have been the one who's been super healthy, I eat well, and so forth. And so, for other people in the family who don't do this stuff, when something happened to me, it was like such a shock it wasn't even funny. It opened everybody at another level much more deeply.*

Tracie: *Wow, that is a blessing. Those are amazing things to be able to bring people into that insight and remind them as a collective, that, you are right, all we have is now and what we do in that moment is precious. It's something we all need to pay attention to.*

We do have another caller so I am going to let you finish and when you are ready for it, let me know.

Nancy: *I am done, go right ahead with the caller.*

Tracie: *Caller what is your question? 'I want to talk about a relationship, a friendship relationship. Is it going to be mended, is it going to come through for Christmas and all that?'*

So, Nancy, do you get any information on that?

Nancy: *Yes, I do. The first thing that I got was, I will tell you from my relationships and give you an example. In my relationships, when the relationship has gone wrong, it has been me, because I chose to view it as something other than it was. So, I had to pull back and look at what I was viewing the relationship as and then decide did I want to make amends, did I want to have that person, that dynamic in my life and continue, or did I want to step back and let it be and let it see what unfolded. Because I found that at different points in my life, some relationships were no longer appropriate for me. We had outgrown each other and the way that we separated was to get mad at one another over one thing or another thing, but the truth of the matter was spiritually we had outgrown one another. Spiritually, we needed to go separate ways and I needed to find people who were more at my spiritual level. The other person needed to find people who were at the spiritual level they were at. Eventually, I came to the understanding that there is no right or wrong, it was simply that we had moved to different places within ourselves and we could no longer maintain the relationship we had. We either each had to make a change or we had to go our separate ways. And sometimes each person changed and we continued on, but the majority of the time, people weren't willing to change or I wasn't willing to stay in the same place. So, it looks like you are going to have to make a decision in yourself as to whether you want to continue in the same vein. Because it appears that the other person isn't necessarily willing at this point in time to change. You are going to have to make a decision, do you want to stay at that level and keep that level of a bit of chaos, a bit of up and down, or do you want to move on and move to a higher level and have a relationship that has less chaos and more stability for you.*

Cherry: *I am going to step in here now also and I was getting the same thing as Nancy. Does this relationship serve you anymore and it is really time for you to look. And it feels as if you are doing your best to hold onto the past. There is a part of you that is doing your best to get approval. If you can create and hold this relationship, then you have won approval. It is very good for you to start looking inside and start loving yourself. I also got, the only way that this relationship is going to continue, is if you are the one to reach out. Even then, you may find it doesn't move in the direction you are hoping it will. You deserve a lot more and this is the reason it is coming up. You are starting to look at what you have in your life and what you want in your life, and what you deserve in your life. It is bringing you to this point so you will do a self-evaluation and find that you deserve so much more in life. I hope that helped. Thank you for calling.*

Tracie: *Okay, so we do have a question in the chat room, and Nancy this is directed to you as it is still related to our subject. Caller says, I had a car wreck where my head smashed through the windshield and two hypoglycemic seizures from diabetes, in all of them I woke up in the ambulance on the way to the hospital. I don't remember anything but the EMTs asking me 'who is the President' when I woke up. Any thought on why I am still here; what is it I need to learn yet?*

Nancy: *You are still here because you are doing Divine work daily. There is a part of your physical body I don't know if it is your eyes or the way you speak, that is actually transmitting out to humanity. And people will comment on that part of your body and notice it and say things to you. And that is why you are here. I want to encourage you not to worry about knowing why you are here, but know that you are here for Divine purpose.*

Focus every single day on knowing that everything you do, think, and say is sacred; that you are here as a Divine Sacred Being. There is something about your eyes that the way you look at people, you look inside of them and you activate something inside them that brings them to a little higher level. Also, the way you speak to people brings a feeling like soothing arms enfolding them. Trust that you don't need to know what you are doing. You don't want to know either because, from my experience, I did know at a point what I was doing with everybody. It was overwhelming; I mean, I could see people's everything, and I asked that it be blocked. I said I just want to do my work, I don't need to know specifically what I am doing for other people because it is too much. So, know that you don't need to know, but you are, in fact, changing many, many people's lives. Not only people's lives, but you are changing the landscape around you, the animals, the birds, you are changing so much around you. So, do not fret about knowing.

Tracie: *Cherry, will you please share the answer you gave him.*

Cherry: *Yes, I will. This is what is lovely about having several readers, because we pick upon different aspects and one of the things that I notice is the diabetes in your life. There is a very common belief system that diabetes actually represents lack of joy in someone's life, lack of sweetness, and I do get you are here also, on the human walk, to remember love, to remember the joys of life, to remember the positives of life. You weren't finished yet, and where Nancy's talking about what you are doing, it is remembering that you are having an energy exchange also that you are not in full awareness of it. When we do this many times we pick up other people's energy, their neediness. We will absorb it into our bodies and so one of the things that would be good for you to heal is to allow yourself to be able to release energies that you are picking up from others. Let me give an example. Because years ago, I didn't understand I had many.... All of a sudden, I had a dream and I had a Being next to me and they showed me this woman and she had unending sadness in her eyes. I thought to myself, why would anyone choose a life of unending sadness. Then the Being had me look again and it showed me the same woman only she was sitting on a hill and all of a sudden, this beauty, this light was coming from her eyes and just absolute love. In front of her was this energy of peace and golden light. It was just flowing from her. I thought, oh my gosh, she is transmuting energy, and then the Being pointed to me. This is where Nancy was talking about how people are drawn to you and they show their arms wrapped around you, you are actually pulling in their energy and yet, you are not allowing it to leave. So, when you feel the heaviness, feeling the lack of positives, the lack of joy, whether it is yours or someone else's, ask your angels or your essence to assist you in transmuting the energy that you are carrying, or have carried, into love and let it leave the physical body, your physical Beingness. Yes, you are doing your job but you are also here to experience love and joy in the physical world. Your eyes light up with light and love.*

Tracie: *What I was getting for you, everything Nancy and Cherry have been saying is spot on. What I want to add to that is unconditional love. It feels to me like you have been experiencing love under conditions in this and other lifetimes, whether you are the one who is giving those conditions or the other person is the one. Part of the experience is to open up and love without conditions. Now unconditional love to ex-partners, to people around you, co-workers, everything, and let go of judgment and be in the love of what is and know that is perfect.*

And we are out of time. We give a big thank you to Nancy.

Nancy: *Thank you for having me, it was great fun.*

Some of the latter part of the show was not related to my Death experience, but was educational so I thought I would include it.

CHAPTER 5
The Journey Back Into the Physical

When I came back to my body in the ER, I was in an altered state for some time. It was as though this was happening to someone else, yet I knew it was my body. I remember on the 45-minute ambulance ride down to Sutter General Hospital in Roseville that I felt strange and not of my body, yet in my body. If I would have crossed back over at any point, it would have been fine. This state continued until my sister, Barbara, walked into the room the next afternoon. Then I came back into my body more fully. I knew one of the reasons I returned was to be with her until she crosses over. I asked Spirit for her to crossover before me as I know I am better able to handle life without her than she is without me.

The next morning at 10:00 am, Dr. Fehrenbacher implanted a Pacemaker. Barbara arrived around 3:00 pm. When I saw her beautiful face, it drew me back into my body. I knew she would watch over me and I could rest in this reality. She saw that I was well cared for and had foods that I needed. Most of all she stayed with me until I was able to go home a couple of days later. I encouraged her to go stay at my house in Auburn as it is only a 20-minute drive. She wanted to stay at a motel near the hospital so she could spend more time with me.

I came home on Thanksgiving afternoon and was so happy to be home. My precious little Reggie came home as soon as I got there. He was so traumatized that he just came and lay by me. He wasn't his usual bouncy, running, jumping little self. When I am gone, I call him every evening to tell him I love him and that I will be home soon. I couldn't call him and talk to him on the phone while I was in the hospital as I knew I would start sobbing and that would upset him. It took him a couple of months to stop being so anxious. If I went to the bathroom, he would follow me and stay until I was done. He followed me everywhere, watching over me. He is my Temple Guardian, sent to me by Spirit.

There are specific animals that are sent to assist us with our evolution, such as with our emotions or to comfort us in times of distress. The species doesn't matter - four legged, winged, fins, or crawling. They may wake us up when we oversleep, play with us when we are upset, angry or too serious, be our companions on our journey in this life, require us to pet them to learn to love more unconditionally, assist us in our disability, or for a myriad of other reasons. I call these animals Temple Guardians, meaning they are the guardians of the temple of our souls while we are on Earth.

I was living in North Las Vegas when he came to me. I had been looking at the Animal Foundation dogs up for adoption for about a month. One afternoon I saw his little face on the site and read all about him. He had been found wandering in an industrial area all matted and malnourished. They had groomed him and taken his picture looking down at his little face. I thought he was a very small dog. I called them as soon as I saw his face to ask if he had been adopted. They said no, and I said I would be down first thing in the morning and asked when they opened. They said 8:30 am, so Bill and I went down. When they brought him out, he pee-peed all over my legs as he stood upon his hind legs. He had this long body and, I thought, I have a long body. We are a match. I adopted him right then and took him home, and made an appointment with the vet to have him checked over. The vet said he was about 9-10 months old, rather than over a year that the adoption folks said, and that with good care he would be fine. He has been my faithful companion ever since.

As it was Thanksgiving, Barbara and I were longing for turkey, dressing, mashed potatoes, gravy, and all the other things that go with that meal. Shortly after we got home, there was a call from my neighbors, Pete and Janet Dufour, wanting to know if we would like some dinner. They brought over two plates loaded with all we had been wanting. When they had dessert, they brought over two pieces of pumpkin pie with whipped cream. Such loving thoughtfulness at our time of need was greatly appreciated.

After I came home, I felt deeply peaceful, yet had a great deal of trouble balancing my physical body and my emotions. My physical heart hurt, my bones hurt, my body didn't feel right, I didn't want to be here, and I was very depressed after being immersed in pure love in The Light, then coming back to a lower vibration. Barbara was staying with me and I would cry easily and get upset. I strongly felt I didn't want to be alone any more. I contemplated moving near family immediately; a friend encouraged me not to be rash. Enfolded in the pure love of my family, friends, The Council, and Source on the Other Side was still with me. Barbara's soothing energy helped me calm down and was a great comfort to me. She stayed with me for two weeks, which greatly improved the rate at which I healed. She knows intuitively what I am feeling and is there for me without a word.

She did everything from walking Reggie, to cooking, cleaning, washing, shopping, personal things for me, and calling my family and friends to give them updates on my progress. For years I have called her an Earth Angel as she took care of the folks before they crossed over and many others as well. She is firmly planted on the Earth, yet intuitively knows what is needed and when. She is a quiet, gentle, unassuming person with a wealth of creativity, intelligence, and common sense. Her sense of humor is keen and very clever. I missed her a great deal after she left.

CHAPTER 6

Messages from Home

A week after Barbara went home, my friend Cherry Divine came to stay with me for a week and this helped enormously. I had other friends who volunteered to come to stay with me for as long as I needed them. Their genuine open hearts and loving offers, helped me re-center and not feel so lonely. Barbara and I talk with each other frequently and that is a great comfort. My other friends call every week or text, or email me. When I was able to go into deep meditation, I connected with Spirit and that filled my heart and soul. Slowly the heart wrenching loneliness eased.

Because I was in pain on many levels and wasn't getting clear information directly, I called Cherry to ask what was really going on with my body. I do not let myself stay in an unhealthy, unhappy or unenlightened place for long. I know it is important to keep myself in a happy, healthy, open place. Here is what she channeled:

"My first question yesterday is why is the body having so much trouble balancing and that is what it is."

"It is as if the energies were so high when you left and came back it is giving the body difficulty in repairing and in some changes, and it does show the bones meshing back together again. So, I am asking what we can do to balance it because one of the things I know is that the energy I carry can actually create difficulties in the bone structure. And so, this is one of the things that has been an issue with the higher energies off and on as the physical bodies

aren't at a level to contain the vibrational rate that has come in. I get that you are going to a restore point in which it is easier to actually balance the energy in the body and allow it to mend at a quicker pace. It is out there a little bit, it is still coming."

"You are going through progressive work. Each night when you go into the dream state you are actually going into progressive work. So, one of the things we need to do and make it very aware, and they are aware of this, when I say they, it is those assisting us to take care with the physical body. Oh, this is the big reason your doctor said to eat at will because weight actually does help at times when there has been a huge energy surge. It allows more cellular structure that absorbs waters and holds waters for the frequency acclimation. So that is part of it. That is one of the reasons the physical doctors stepped in and said we want you to go ahead and eat at will. You will put on a few poundages but not that much. It will fall away when it is not necessary for you any longer."

"Again, the physical body still has restrictions, so to just have even one more layer around helps. This doesn't have to be a thick layer, but another layer around actually allows the energy to be held more peacefully in the body."

"The thing is even if you put on another 3 or 4 pounds it isn't going to hurt at this point. As a matter of fact, it is actually better for you. It isn't that you are going to get real heavy because you are not, but having that extra layer adds more cells, it's physical cells in the body. Those cells will absorb water and assist because what's happening when you get a surge of energy, think of an electrical current. When the electrical current comes in, it depletes or uses up all water."

"The body is 90% water, so it goes in and kind of sucks you dry so this allows you to have a better foundation for the vibration. A better foundation for the vibrational transference that have been in effect. One of the reasons you have felt depleted in the last 6 to 8 months is because you have been going through a vibrational transference. Now we say "transference" as it is a rate that is at a different level than you are accustomed to upon Earth and in its reality. So again, it brings it up to a stronger point. *The body needs to have assistance in sustaining itself while this process is going on. Understand that it is to balance your core point and you are in agreement with this, that it is something you said yes, you would accommodate. It is necessary for this time period on Earth."*

"Again, and when you did what you call the crossing over, or in truth, the communication board (I call The Council) that you met with, we are using terms that are easy to be understood in the reality of mankind. You had a meeting point that was to be occurring at that time. It was necessary to step out of the body because, in truth, if you would have stayed in the body, it would not have been able to be brought back and be useful. And it is very important that you have chosen to be useful in this particular life. It is not to say that you will be going off gung ho into the world, but you are holding a particular energy that does assist in the changes that are occurring here in the Western Hemisphere. Again, this is where you have chosen to localized and to restore, but we ask that you have patience with the body. It is asked that you not give up and not to allow the emotions to overrun. We are assisting in an emotional balance – this is also throwing you out of alignment making it less easy for you to absorb the changes. It is to understand that what you choose to have occur in your daily life and what it is you choose to have present in your life as a whole is your choice. But understand that underneath the workings of this is a migratory vibrational frequency. This is to assist in the balancing in this particular hemisphere."

"There are others that are in pinpoints of other destinations that you are assisting with. This is important to understand. We are using words of mankind and they are not fully accurate in meanings, but in the meanings, you will have more understanding. As you listen back to this just allow this to go in and not to be thought hard on, but just to allow the inner messages to be broadcast throughout you. For this will also assist in the mending of the physical body."

"You had to adjust your timeline for the changes on the timeline of Planet Earth."

"You will notice there is a shift in your eyesight. It will come in streams and then it will seem to go out in wavy elements, yet it will again balance itself. There is much work going on within you; it is to remember this is a time process and so you will have minor irritations, but not to be overwhelmed by those."

"There you go, it shows you being as if there is energy that keeps coming into you in this area and that is why you were guided to Auburn. You have been guided several places – Corvallis, Las Vegas, and then here to Auburn. And each time you are a conduit of energy and then it showed people standing at other poles within the world and you are all carrying this in helping to hold this energy. It is going through the Earth plates; but it is also the inner cities that are assisting with this balancing. It is like, you are almost like generator stones, that is what they are showing. It shows the inner earth, then the top layer of earth, then the outside of earth."

"O my gosh there is just a lot going on in the crown chakra right now. You might just all of a sudden feel it because – in the crown chakra particularly. Is your hair changing color? "

(I answered, yes, it was turning white at the crown.)

"Exactly, mine too, and I have been working to restore that. Very, very white, just in the crown chakra. You can see dark strands go back into it so that the hair pulls in the color again but it has to do with the energy. Mine did a big circle of just white, white hair right at the crown. And that has to do with the energy that is being carried and anchored in. But it shows those above us, it shows us and then it shows the inner cities."

"And that's it; the body is having a little difficulty but they are restoring that. And that is one of the things is not to become overwhelmed or over worried when these happen, just keep up on the physical level with the different things and that will assist."

"And what is really fun here is I play with energy at the top of my head – Gawd, this is going really white and so I just saw dark strands of hair coming up and going through and it actually changed the *color of my hair and it is streaking now through my hair. It is much darker now than my hair has ever been."*

"So that is something to understand that the energy that is coming from can recolor your hair without processing. So that was interesting. Again, it waffles back and forth whether it will hold, but it is interesting to watch it happen."

(I just asked that the hair color that is the most appropriate for my skin and for myself be brought back in.)

"Continue your morning walk and exercise as you can, and walk again in the afternoon or early evening. Again, the walking movement; there is a limitation on this for just a brief period of time with the rib."

(One morning I had woken up to find out my rib was broken.)

"But you will find that you will go back to dancing and that is one of the reasons you were there."

(I had been taking Ballroom Dance Lessons.)

"It allows the mind to move off into a different direction, but it also gives the body the necessary exercise. When you get tired just go ahead and stop. You need the interaction with people; it brings you mentally to a lower emotional point. So that when you are there and participating, even though it is the same old, same old, it actually allows your vibration to rise emotionally because there is connection and interaction and unity. Do what you can to interact with other people because the emotions somehow blindfold you to all of the agreements that you have."

(I said I would.)

(I said I see no companion on the horizon around here.)

"There is one there for you. They are saying that you and I are very good at perfecting the art of what is wrong with what is around

us when it comes to the male species. And that is why it is insisting that we look outside of what we know and to let go of the old beliefs and judgments. I don't know why I was guided to go to different cultures, Japanese, Black, Hispanic, etc., because I have never really done this sort of thing, but it helps us to remember to release our mental blockages and to look at the old programs we have running through us."

"Then once we open doors, that doesn't mean that that will be the person or nationality we go with, but we will move through limiting thoughts. And it is like me looking at (his name), he is short, not all that attractive, but, damn, he is sweet. And that is so that I look at my personal projections and judgments."

(I said I am doing that with some of the people at dance.)

"The more that we let go of this, it doesn't mean that will be the person that is our life partner, but it actually opens the doorway for the life partner. Again, it is not to give up hope because you have had somebody that is very close to you – they are saying they are readying the front. It is like they are opening an entry point. They say you left the wailing wall and are now marching onto a new pathway. Oh, the grief at the wall, okay you have left the grief at the wall, now you are opening your heart."

(My husband of 45 years died June 3, 2014 and I have been grieving.)

After I was given this information, I was able to tolerate the changes my body, mind, and emotions underwent with greater ease of all my bodies. I am deeply grateful to Cherry for her ability to truly be an open channel and for her clarity of connection and information.

CHAPTER 7
Adjusting to Earth Life

Debbie Smith, another incredible Medium, also channeled my husband, Bill, after he crossed over bringing in a different perspective on information about things going on. This was extremely helpful to me. She helped me select the home I presently live in as Spirit knew it would be the better home for me. She also helped me hold to the price I wanted to pay as she knew the seller was needing to get out of the home.

Debbie brought through the information that I was to write this book and some other books. She continually encourages me in all ways with her joyful manner and her delightful humor. She especially encourages me to write my books. She is connecting my book, *My Spiritual Journey and Yours*, with Japanese readers. I love her so much and know we will continue to be part of each other's lives. It humbles me that I am so blessed to have her in my life to help me move faster, easier, and with precise information. I have paraphrased channeling from Debbie in this chapter.

When I came back in, I was told that this was my last exit point and that I was here for the duration. I was told I would be pretty close to triple digits by the time I go. I also was told that my health would be fine until the day I crossed over, that I would be alert, functioning, and independent the whole time. This was important information as it makes it easier for me to go forward with life here and my spiritual work. I couldn't be wasting time with illness or things of that nature as I had already had those experiences early in this life and in other lives. I am here to hold the Light energies, vibrations and frequencies and to teach others. I knew I would be assisting people to understand things that were going on in the world from a different perspective so they could grow.

The death process triggered more awareness in my mind. My energy body increased, and when something resonates with me, I am able to focus on it and manifest the outcome. I check periodically about my nutrition and the vitamins I take. After my return, my body is able to better draw more out of the vitamins and nutrition I give it and it responds better to them.

A couple of months after I returned from the Other Side, I had scheduled two classes to teach. I did all the flyers, email lists, etc., however my vibration was so high, people who normally would have come did not as they could not connect with my vibrational level. It was as though I was invisible. I knew that they would come back at some point when their own level was higher or I bring mine to a level lower to accommodate them. My Spirit would not be held away from doing this. I had the awareness that I needed to care for the physical body in a way that I had not before. The higher Light energies, vibrations, and frequencies that would be used during the events would require me to take extra care of the physical body.

Because my body was in an adjustment and restoration state, I rested before and after these classes. In my everyday life, integrating the higher level Light energies, vibrations and frequencies requires me to stop and rest at various times. I will be doing something and get so sleepy, that I need to lay down or recline in my chair. A half hour or an hour later, I am wide awake and ready to go. It seems to come to me in waves. It has continued since I returned and will be ongoing.

Writing certain parts of this book required me to stop and rest as I am connecting with and bringing in information of a higher level that changes my Light energies, vibrations and frequencies when it is in me. It is exhilarating to be this altered state as I feel totally alive in every cell of my body and am expanded in ways it is difficult to describe.

I spoke earlier about not wanting to be alone. Bill had told me he would send me someone so I wouldn't be alone. I reached a point during my restoration, that I just said I won't be alone any longer. I want a life partner and I want him now. Well, you know how that works or doesn't work. I wasn't ready for a life partner physically, emotionally, mentally, and probably spiritually was the only way I thought I was ready. I was still grieving the death of my beloved husband of 45 years.

Part of the death process and infusion on the other side was the designing of a life with a partner, the changes within myself that were going to be made, and the actual manifestation of a mate. When I am ready, I will attract someone who is able to support me on various levels and who is accepting of my spiritual work. Working with beings from other realms screens many men out as they have no understanding that this is a normal activity for human beings.

The rhythm of the electrical circuitry of my heart had not been in full force. I had so little physical energy, I would rest after breakfast and off and on during the day. The Pacemaker had to be calibrated by the Light Surgeons from the higher planetary elevations to come and assist with the configuration of the Pacemaker instrument that has been placed within my heart. My heart is more than a physical instrument for my physical body; it contains a Light Essence of love that is sent out to humanity. It draws to me my life partner when I am ready and others as it is time for them to come into my life. Previously, Cherry Divine suggested I visualized pure Divine Golden Light intertwining with Pure Divine Royal Blue Light coming from Source down through my heart out to my life partner and back up to Source. I asked that our connection to be from, of, and through the Divine.

In March of 2017, I flew down to see Barbara as I wanted to be close to her and rest in the warm Arizona sun. We had a wonderful, leisure time and it filled my heart with warmth and my body with more healing. The trip was a bit stressful for me, yet I unpacked, did the wash, went to the store, took care of Reggie, ate dinner, and did everything I wanted to get done. Later that night, I had an episode with my heart where I felt like I was going to faint, my body started to lose liquids and solids. My Pacemaker kicked in and I went to bed. I felt better in the morning. I had to learn to slow down for a while. Spirit reminded me that the heart is a human organ, and while I love to live in the Spirit world, I need to be mindful of the limitations of the human body and pace myself.

I have a St. Jude Medical Merlin Home Transmitter by my bed that monitors my heart through the night, and sends signals to my Cardiologist's Office. Neither the machine nor my Pacemaker were going off, yet I had an episode where my heart wasn't acting right. It happened while Cherry was visiting. I could not figure out what was going on, so asked Cherry to see if she could. She got that it was the crystals I had by the bed, specifically the Copper and Hematite stones. The magnetic charge in these stones was effecting my heart. I went to www.HealingCrystals.com, and found an article that stated in answer to the question: "Are crystals safe for a Pacemaker?" "You want to avoid any crystals that have a magnetic charge – two specific ones are Hematite and Shungite. The magnetic charge in genuine Hematite is fairly low but you want to be safe as it is best to avoid Hematite as well as any other crystals that might contain traces of Hematite (Tire Iron, Iron Jasper, etc.)." They referred me to a link titled "Crystal Safeguards". It was very enlightening. In addition to keeping my Pacemaker away from my cell phone, any large generator charges, massive electrical lines, etc., I now had to watch the crystals I have in my home. Fascinating!

The other thing that Cherry picked up was the remote-control devices on my nightstand. The two remotes sitting on my nightstand were also sending currents to my heart. One was for my bed to raise and lower, and the other was for the TV. Both were sending out strong enough currents to affect the heart instrument. So, I removed the stones and the remotes.

A few nights later, the Pacemaker went off for about five minutes a while after I went to bed. It surprised me as I was feeling great all day. I was telling Cherry about it the next morning and she said I was going too far out of my body. Every night when I go to bed, I go out to continue my spiritual work at night. I asked The Council to assist me in assuring my body was caused no distress during my night journeys. If someone had told me I would be doing this, thinking about these things, and have Spirit living through me, I would have thought they were loco. It brings me great joy in my life and I am so grateful.

Some family members and friends have trouble sleeping; I have none. I know why I don't have any problem sleeping. When I go to bed, I go to sleep immediately. My body rests and renews itself and my Spirit goes to wherever it is called. Such a beautiful joining of the two worlds. Debbie brought me the information that the Other Side told me I needed to stay in at least three nights, rather than going out every night. I just answer the call.

While it was healing, my body had blood pressure issues, low blood pressure, where I had no energy and felt dizzy at times. I was not getting enough blood flow and oxygen to the organs. When I went to the doctor I was told to eat more salt and eat more food. I love Lays Potato Chips, so this was a great treat to be told to eat more salty things. I have always watched what and how much I eat, so it was delightful to be told to eat more food. I promptly went out and had a steak with mashed potatoes and country gravy, vegetables, biscuits with gravy, and ice cream for dessert. A delicious celebration dinner! I brought half of it home for the next day as I was unaccustomed to eating that much food. But it was fun.

I was also told to start getting more exercise just walking around the house, in the yard, and down one block and back. Before my heart stopped, I was used to getting up, exercising, taking Reggie for a walk, then going about my day. During my walk, I connect with Spirit and I am infused for the day. When my heart stopped, all the exercise stopped to allow my body to heal. I knew Spirit was there, but I was focused on my physical body healing.

In April when my body started feeling better, I began to work on getting out my book, *My Spiritual Journey and Yours*. I had finished it in December 2016. I had to consciously work through the constrictions and restrictions that had been a part of my childhood and life to this point. In the past, I only allowed myself to be a little successful. Now I am opening to allow myself to be totally successful and to be joyful doing it, plus I opened up to receiving lots of money. I trust that my book will go to whoever is meant to have it and I will be richly rewarded in many ways. I trust that I will be successful beyond my wildest dreams. A gift from my trip to the Other Side is this certainty within. Such a rare and precious gift!

During the latter part of April and the first part of May, my heart was hurting and I felt a physical heaviness. I wondered if my heart was slowing down again or my blood pressure was low, or some other thing. In talking with Debbie Smith, she faced me with the deep grief that I had suppressed when Bill died. It was delayed and that is why my heart hurt so much. I was strong for everybody during this time, taking care of death details, the children and grandchildren, and the Celebration of Life Service, selling the Las Vegas house, looking for property, and then moving to Auburn, CA. My heart was fine physically; it was emotionally hurting with grief for my beloved husband. Debbie encouraged me to take some time and go deeper as this would free up the blocked energy. Once the block is removed, it opens a path for a life partner if I so choose.

Quite a while back, I asked for help with staying in balance. Debbie brought through the information that my Other Side family, friends, The Council and all who work with this level of Light energy, vibration and frequency "feed my balance." They feed my physical, mental, emotional, spiritual, Light body, and the essence of my Beingness. It is a Light Stream that flows to me with fine threads of what is needed. With the feeding comes wisdom and information that quickly lets me know the why of the imbalance, the way to re-balance, and prevention of future imbalances. It is transmitted to me as a "knowing" or a picture in my mind, or if the need is urgent, it is done automatically. Sometimes it comes through another source, such as a Medium, song, words, etc., that stand out in printed form. For instance, a book title will appear to me to be much larger than it actually is, and I will know this is a personal message for me, or that I am to buy that book. Someone will say something to me in a normal tone of voice and I hear it louder. It is so comforting to know that I am being fed to keep my balance in ways known and unknown to me. Spirit's priceless treasures are of such unimaginable magnitude!

It is June now and I am back integrating all the changes that I experienced and that are ongoing. My connection with the Other Side remains strong. I am enfolded each morning when I meditate before I get up, so the longing to return Home is manageable. The love I feel inside myself and for All That Is overwhelms me at times and makes me cry at the beauty of it.

CHAPTER 8

Healing Abilities

I entered this life with healing abilities. As a child, and up until adulthood, there was an unconscious knowing that I worked with others to heal them. When I became an adult, I would know I was healing others. This was helpful during my career and in daily life as I would know what was needed in a situation to resolve most problems or keep them from becoming a problem. I am a vessel for Spirit to bring Light energies, vibrations, and frequencies through. Spirit does it all!

Before Exit 1999, I was aware that my healing abilities were pretty good. After I came back from my check in on the Other Side, I noticed that my healing abilities improved in both ability and speed. I didn't keep track of people I worked on at that time, so don't have records of the work I did. The following is one memory I have of a healing I (Spirit) did.

The healing occurred when I was with a church group outing on Mount Shasta. One of the women couldn't participate with the group because she had a terrible headache and backache. I asked if I could work on her and she said yes. After I sent Light throughout all of her Beingness for a few minutes, she was healed instantly. It surprised me that it was so quick. At times, it takes days, months, or more for the healing to be completed because of the person's condition, willingness, the extent of the work done, or other factors.

After Exit 2016, my healing abilities are markedly different. When I think of someone who would benefit from assistance, I send Light and know this has helped them. I observe events that I want to happen in my own life unfold, step by step, without any effort on my part. I observe and experience changes in family and friends, as well as events at large in the world when I send Light and/or ask for help from the Other Side. In some instances, healing occurs instantaneously and I am awed by what is happening.

In addition to my daily prayers, I use Light as a healing, transmuting, activating, and transformative force. For instance, when I see something on TV, see an animal on the roadside, hear an argument, or any number of other things, I send Pure Divine Light. Spirit knows my intention.

I want to tell you more about the "Light" I use in healing and journey sessions. Most of you are familiar with laser surgery now, which is the use of intense light. In *The Bible*, God, Jesus, and the Apostles, as well as lay people, speak about Light's use and its transformative powers. Many people do not understand that many parts of *The Bible* are channeled by what were called Prophets at that time, and are called Mediums today. Some scholars say that the original words and meaning of *The Bible* have been changed over the centuries by man according to man's desires. I encourage you to read *The Bible* from cover to cover as it is very enlightening.

A while back I read a book entitled *Dancing with Water: The New Science of Water* by M. J. Pangman, MS and Melanie Evans. In it the authors quote Dr. Fritz Albert Popp, the modern German scientist well-known for his work with biphotonic energy. He states:

"We know today that man is essentially a being of light. We now know for example that light can initiate, or arrest cascade-like reactions in the cells, and that genetic cellular damage can be virtually repaired within hours, by faint beams of light. We are still on the threshold of fully understanding the complex relationship between light and life, but we can now say emphatically, that the function of our entire metabolism is dependent on light."

It was shown to me how the negativity of humanity effects the weather systems and many more things than one can imagine. Negative residue reverberates out into the Cosmos and is transmuted into love and returned to the Earth and those thereon. We here on Earth are responsible for creating and holding the Light energies, vibrations, and frequencies of love. I encourage you to bring Light into yourself and then to send Light when you see something that disturbs or upsets you. Just think the word "Light" and observe what happens.

In 2002, Bill and I were guided to move to Corvallis, Oregon. We opened Sacred Healing, LLC, and began doing healing work in Oregon. We had healing circles and did private individual healing. We attended fairs and expos to expand our work. It was so deeply rewarding to work on everyone from a non-English speaking person to a medical doctor as well as observe and receive reports of the results. The following are some of the more memorable Recent Events, Testimonials, and Case Histories.

Recent Events

In 2016 an individual came to me for a private Sacred Journey Session. The person had an immune disorder that the medical community was treating. The individual had other issues and had been unable to work due to the medical condition and these issues. The immune disorder required a body device so injections could be made directly into the system. This person was worked on once or twice a month for four months. During this time, the device was removed, the other issues were resolved satisfactorily, and the person became employed full time. Divine Light was used to do the healing along with intuitive recommendations from Spirit. A beautiful example of Western Medicine, Spirit healing and intuitive messages working together.

For about 20 years I had ever worsening arthritis in my hands. I got steroid shots but they stopped working. However, I was able to go this long because Nancy did perform healing on my hands. I did have surgery on my hands, one at a time, and Nancy sent healing energy each time. My surgeon was amazed at how quickly it healed and how little pain I had. She kept telling me to "take it easy, don't use them so much", but I used them as soon as the casts came off. I attribute this to Nancy and Spirit!

— 2017 Debbie S, WA

Sacred Healing Testimonials

A medical doctor, age 45 or so came to me for assistance with her body and with a relationship issue. Spirit worked on the body and the issue resolved. She had been having difficulty drawing someone to her that would be a loving life partner/spouse. Spirit outlined the steps she needed to take. She came back to me a few months later, saying that she had met the man of her dreams and was going to marry him. They were married and are living happily in another state. She thanked me and I thanked Spirit.

As soon I met Nancy and Bill, I felt my life would become peaceful. Every time I need a session with Nancy, she cures my mind and after that she cures my whole physical body. I have been seeing them for three years. My life has changed for the better.

— Blanca Nunez, Corvallis, Oregon

Case Histories and Outcomes

Enrique came for a private session complaining of stomach pain and kidney pain. He was under a doctor's care and taking medication, but not improving. Nancy did a healing on him and he had immediate relief from the kidney pain and the stomach pain diminished slightly. Enrique attended the healing group for about a year. He had another session with Nancy and another healer, and all pain was removed. During that session, he reported that he saw light, and a dime materialized on his shirt at the end of the session. Enrique was surprised and grateful.

— Subject: Enrique Alvarado, Corvallis, Oregon
Witnessed by Blanca Nunez, translator

Cruz Medina, 18 years old, was unjustly arrested as a result of a relative accusing him of something he did not do. Blanca called Nancy, explained the situation and Nancy began doing light work for truth and justice to prevail. His first three months in jail, he felt someone was working on him because he saw the light that Nancy was putting on him. He had faith that everything was going to be cleared up. I believe the light work that Nancy did cleared all the paperwork and two months later, the judge decided that Cruz was innocent. He was released one month later.

— Subject: Cruz Medina, Durango, Mexico
(Blanca Nunez, translator)

Adelia had been sick for about three years and the only part that the doctors picked up from her was the blood was not right for her body. They were doing a transfusion every six months and she was feeling the same. Blanca called Nancy to ask if she would help her and immediately Nancy began doing light work for her. The minute Nancy put the light on her, she saw that she was almost dead. Adelia received all the energy her body could hold at the time, and the first day she felt relief. Adelia was worked on steadily for four weeks and she was healed and no longer needed transfusions. Her healing work was done remotely by viewing a photograph.

— Adelia Villanueva, El Toro, California
(Blanca Nunez, translator)

I began attending Nancy and Bill Waldron's weekly healing and energy meditation group sessions more than two years ago. Our weekly energy and healing sessions clear and balance my mind and spirit and have healed many things in my body.

The most recent experience was quite significant. I have restrictive lung disease and other problems. For years I have suffered stomach and intestinal pain and discomfort. After three local doctors examined me, I was referred to a specialist. He performed an ultrasound and it revealed matter that indicated pre-gallstones, plus blockage in my bile duct. He told me the next step was a surgical procedure that would require me to undergo general anesthesia. I had a near-death experience the last time I had general anesthesia, and I know it is life-threatening to me. My choice was take the risk and live out my days with a breathing tube or try for one month to take a medication three times a day and have follow up ultrasound and see where we stood.

I left the specialist's office with a prescription. That evening, I talked with my children about the prognosis and they gave me their blessings on whatever I chose to do. Then I prayed and meditated and called Nancy. She suggested we do weekly healing sessions during the month I was taking the medication. After talking to her, I prayed and meditated again and fell asleep. During the night, in a vision, the doctor and Nancy both appeared in full body form. We discussed every aspect of the situation and they vanished. I sat on the edge of my bed and played it over in my mind and then totally surrendered myself to Divine Spirit. When I woke in the morning, I knew exactly what I was going to do—I was going to take the medicine and follow the procedure and leave it up to God.

I completed three sessions with Nancy and Bill, and they were deep and profound and cleansing. During the second session, I felt the energy of the entities enter and felt their energy moving through my body to the diseased parts. I was fully conscious, and I could feel it. The light energy remained with me for more than two weeks and I totally surrendered to it. The third session was like a refresher. I had a knowing that told me not to go to the fourth healing session until I knew to go. Before that happened, the 30 days ended and I went back to doctor for another ultrasound.

Three or four days later, a cheerful doctor called me with the results. He was almost yelling because he was so excited to report *good news to a patient: "It is gone—all traces of the matter are completely gone!" he said.*

I rejoiced with him, my family, and Nancy and Bill, and I shared this whole story with the group. The pure power of Nancy and Bill's energy and how they surrender to our Divine Spirit to be used to heal, help, and guide us is a priceless gift in my life. When I am in their presence, I feel their luminous energy and feel that I am with people whose soul intention is pure. That is such a rare experience in our world.

— Carol Parks, Philomath, Oregon

CHAPTER 9

Opportunities

There are so many opportunities to open to Spirit, if you are willing. The benefits far outweigh any perceived societal concerns or judgments of others. My Journey has been on the outer edges of what is perceived by many as "normal." It has taken me to the Other Side and back twice; I would not have missed these opportunities.

During illness or death, Spirit has been my constant companion whether I believed completely or was filled with doubt. I consciously chose to open more, accept more, explore more, and follow my own inner promptings. At times, this went against my husband, family, friends, work associates, society, and religious groups. It was lonely at times as few understood what I felt or knew.

During times of great joy and happiness, Spirit helped me expand and hold these feelings for longer and longer periods of time. Now, my life is joy and happiness the vast majority of time every day no matter is going on. There are no great dips in emotions and large amounts of time where I feel lost and don't know where to turn. I trust completely that there is Divine purpose in every aspect of my life. I do not have to know what that is as it will unfold and be revealed to me if it is mine to know.

You have the opportunity to choose to connect with Spirit in every way. I choose to connect with Spirit through Mediums when I cannot get a clear answer myself. I choose not to sit and wallow in self-pity, self-hatred, self-judgment, and all the other ways I used to do because I didn't know my value as a Divine Being and I didn't know clear answers were available. I choose not to self-medicate with anything, as I used to self-medicate with cigarettes and driving myself to work more, harder.

Every moment, I have the opportunity to embody Spirit. I live Spirit and am so grateful to do that. I am high on life, so I don't need alcohol, drugs, food, cigarettes, or any of the other self-medicating habits available. I don't need attention every minute or most of the time, like I used to. I am happy and content within myself with my little dog, Reggie, and my simple life.

So, I invite you to take the opportunity to open up to Spirit, and/or to find a reputable Medium, take a chance, and change whatever in your life isn't working, or if it is working, to make it work better. It is the most freeing, simple step I ever took with the most profound results. For me, working with a Medium cleared away all of the years of talking in therapy, the religious dogma that was talk, but not walking the talk, the glossing over of real problems and issues to look good, and getting genuine, truthful answers. I felt the "truth" when I heard it; it was a physical sensation that anchored me closer and closer to Spirit.

I invite you to notice the subtle energy, vibrations, and frequencies around you. Notice how you feel when you look at your favorite flower. Notice when your cat or dog comes up to you, the energy they bring. Notice when you hear a voice on the phone how it makes your body feel, the tone, the pitch, the words used, and so forth. Pay attention to how you feel in crowds, small groups, and in gatherings of one or two. Notice if you pick up other people's feelings and energies. Explore information about empaths to find out if you are one, and if so, what kind. These are opportunities to know yourself and others better. These are opportunities to protect yourself from those who feed off of your energy.

For many years, I did not tell anyone what was happening inside me, and that I was going to Mediums. It was too risky with my family and others in my world. If you feel the same way, I invite you to take yourself on a private journey with no one knowing, or only one or two trusted people if you must have support, and find your connection with Spirit and with truth. My experience is that I found far greater, deeper truths in Mediums connecting with Spirit than anywhere else.

Spirit sent me support in many forms, books, cassette tapes, DVDs, classes, workshops, retreats, churches that were on the cutting edge, spiritual groups, personal spiritual mentors, and helped open up family and friends. Take a chance on yourself and your own personal connection with Spirit. Now is a good time.

Silently, privately, every morning and night, ask Spirit to come to you to help you open in ways that are appropriate for you. Ask that you be protected on your journey, that you be guided, and that you be kept in balance. Ask that those you love be opened, if it is in their highest and best good. You do not need to tell anyone you are doing this. Observe what happens in your life and say thank you every time you recognize Spirit at work, no matter how small the progress.

During my journey, I used to swear and damn was my favorite word. One day I noticed that I didn't swear when something happened when I would have used that word. I immediately said thank you and began noticing that I didn't need to use that word at all, as I found my voice with other kinder, clearer words. I still say thank you every time I notice something that Spirit has helped me with. Now it doesn't occur to me to swear daily and when I hear someone else swear, I silently send them Pure Divine White Light. My intent is to help them find other kinder, clearer words. Whether or not they use the Light is up to them.

One of the opportunities that helped me make the choices I have is when a Medium asked me if I wanted to be back here doing the same things over again in my next life. That was like dynamite blasting me off my hesitation, as I did not want to be back doing the same thing the same way.

You will have the opportunity to give yourself permission to let go of what does not work, those who do not support you, or those who bring you down. You will have the opportunity to forgive those who are unable to journey with you, and to choose to forgive within yourself as it releases negative energy from you. Wish them well on their journey and mean it. Your encouragement may make the difference in them choosing a path of Light.

We are each at a different level on our journey and there is no right or wrong, no judgment of good or bad. Of course, in this society on Earth, there is judgment everywhere. We have the opportunity to make a difference by our choices. We are each only where we have opened spiritually at this moment. That could change in an instant. I am responsible for changing myself. By changing myself, I help change everything.

Give yourself the opportunity to assist humanity, the world and the Earth by opening to the precious love of Spirit. It is a gift beyond measure that will change you, those around you, and All That Is.

Always, I hold you in Spirit's Love and Light on your journey.

Epilogue: A Heart Filled with Gratitude

That I have been so blessed throughout my life with people, animals, plants, crystals, the sky, the land, experiences, and the precious Beings with me, is something I give thanks for every day. These beautiful souls, mentioned below, who journeyed with me, in one way or another, fill me with a humbleness and a gratitude at the love they bestow upon me. I am forever grateful to them and for them.

My neighbors, Kal and Heather Jaber made the trip to the Other Side and back possible by their quick action. They are precious beyond words. They comforted and kept my little Reggie dog while I was gone. We are more than neighbors as our hearts are interwoven with love for each other and the journeys we each are taking and sharing. They are extraordinarily brave and courageous people. They have an 8-year old son, Adam, who helped take care of and play with Reggie, and a darling little dog, Teddy, who is Reggie's best friend. I ask that you pray for them and hold them in the Light daily.

My son, Wayne Waldron, had the paper that I had prepared in the event of my illness or death right on hand. He had his wife, Nikki, who is a nurse, call the ER and give them information about medications I was allergic to. She kept checking my status while I was in and out of my body, until my heart stabilized. These two are such beautiful, loving beings. They invited me to stay at their home after going through the transition where my husband died, the Las Vegas home sold, and I found another home. They both comforted me and enfolded me in their love. There is so much more to all that they did and do, I could write pages. They are an integral part of my heart and life, and I love them so much. Wayne is his father's son in every good way. They both make the world a better place.

My sister, Barbara Widner, my Earth Angel, a part of my heart, I cry at the beauty of her love for me and my little dog, Reggie. The beauty of her generous, loving soul is so great it touches me and teaches me. Her lifelong journey beside me, her caring for me during Bill's illness and death, her care of me this time, and her ongoing love of me makes it all worthwhile. May God enfold her with all her heart desires now and forevermore.

I am blessed with incredibly gifted Mediums as friends. Cherry Divine, and I have had a close relationship since we met in Corvallis, Oregon, at a gathering my husband and I were having. Her husband crossed over at 8:00 am, October 9, 2012. Spirit asked me to walk beside her to support her through her grief and I did. When my husband, Bill, was having memory problems, Cherry and another friend would come over to my house to have lunch and connect with Spirit during the afternoon. Bill would sit on the couch and not say much, but would listen to everything we said to each other and what came from Spirit. When it came time for me to move us closer to the children and where it would be less expensive for us, Cherry immediately volunteered to help me drive from Corvallis to Las Vegas. She helped me start to get settled there. She came to visit so I would not be so lonely. Bill died at 2:12 pm on June 3, 2014. She channeled Bill's spirit from the time he crossed over and continues to do so. She met me in Auburn to help me begin to look for property. It made such a difference when I had information on whether a place had major issues, was in a deteriorating neighborhood, was overpriced, or when to let go of a property. She continues to walk beside me and I her. She genuinely supports my spiritual work. We are so blessed to have each other. I am so grateful for the gift of her in my life. She merges with me in Spirit in a way that is unique and leaves me in grateful amazement. I love and am in awe of her beautiful generous soul.

Debbie Smith is the other incredible Medium friend that I have. We met when Bill and I owned Sacred Healing, LLC, in Corvallis, Oregon. We would go to the expos and fairs around Oregon and met Debbie at one of them. She had such loving sweetness about her, such gentle energy, combined with exceptional channeling abilities, that we both loved her immediately. Bill was not one to believe in Mediums; he was skeptical. I got a reading and knew she was special. Then we began exchanging readings and healing. She lives in Gig Harbor, Washington, so we didn't get to see her much, but stayed in contact by phone. She helped me while I was grieving over Bill's death. We continue to assist each other. She carries a very high fine vibration and frequency. She is another Divine Gift to me.

My precious other children and grandchildren, other family members and friends sent flowers, gifts, called, sent cards and letters, as well as emails and texts. For all who offered to come to stay with me from a couple of days to no time limit, your loving offers gave me the courage to keep going as I knew you would be there if I needed you. Each one of you lifted my spirits up and helped me want to remain here on Earth. I thank you for the shower of love, genuine offers of help, and gratitude for my Beingness.

To Sue Crawford, my exceptionally creative and talented friend, website manager, book manager, and good business sense person, you are a gift from Spirit. You make it so easy for me to bring forth what Spirit asks, then you make it presentable for the public, and get it distributed. You are a joy to work with and your love for my little Reggie, warms both our hearts. Thank you from the bottom of my old and new heart. I love you, my dear friend.

To my deceased parents, Walter and Ruth Otte, I thank you for the gift of life, for the many lessons, and for the rich journey we shared. To my sister Patricia S. Newton, thank you for the fun early times in California, for your presence through the ups and downs of life, for the daily calls after my heart issue, and for your continuing deep love as we walk this journey together. You bless me beyond measure. I love you.

To the physical doctors and loving nurses, and to the interplanetary surgeons, specialists, and Beings, I give great thanks for your care of me in and out of the body. Your wisdom, skills, and abilities enlighten and delight us all. I am deeply grateful to you now and forevermore. These words are inadequate; I trust that you know all that I am is yours.

My journeys to the Other Side and return to life are the greatest gifts I have been given.

May each of you be aware of, and allow yourself to feel the love from Source that is available to you each moment.

I love you all.

Nancy A. Waldron

Resources

Mediums Recommended:

Cherry Divine, www.cherrydivine.com

Debbie Smith, www.debbie-smith.net

Radio Show and Host:

Cherry Divine, www.cherrydivine.com

Tracie Mahan, www.traciemahan.com

"Somethin Brewin" Blog Talk Radio Show

Books:

The Bible

The Empath's Survival Guide by Judith Orloff, MD

Dancing with Water: The New Science of Water by M.J. Pangman, MS and Melanie Evans

Websites:

My website, www.nancyawaldron, has other resources listed.

Every Moment

of

Every Day

is

Sacred

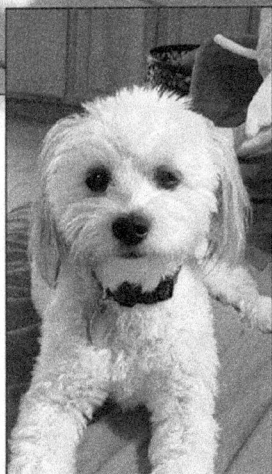

Reggie

Nancy A. Waldron is an author and a spiritual mentor who facilitates Sacred Journey Workshops, Sacred Journey Sessions, and Mount Shasta Spiritual Journeys. She authored *A Joyful Miracle*, written following her Father's death and after her first trip to the Other Side. She authored *My Spiritual Journey and Yours* just prior to her second trip to the Other Side. She authored this book after her second trip to the Other Side.

Nancy was born multi-gifted, and at a young age dedicated her life to the continuous opening to Spirit and to mentoring others. She considers she has a PhD in her personal life experience, both the good and not so good. Her journey took her through therapy, churches, psychics, and healers, as well as a life-long study of spirituality through *The Bible*, many other books, classes, workshops, retreats, and individual sessions with spiritual leaders. This process led her to decide to publicly share her innate spiritual knowing.

She co-owned Sacred Healing, LLC, in Oregon, with her husband, facilitating healing of people and situations in the United States and elsewhere. They facilitated individual healing, and hosted weekly meditation groups and Sacred Healing Circles. She works with people remotely by viewing a photograph, by telephone, in groups, and in person.

Nancy A. Waldron
www.nancyawaldron.com
530.878.5757 | nancyawaldron@aol.com

www.ingramcontent.com/pod-product-compliance
Lightning Source LLC
Chambersburg PA
CBHW072209090426
42740CB00012B/2456